Financial Foundation System

Helping Middle America Eliminate Debt & Maximize Savings

Table of Contents

Introduction:

About Me:

I0504872

Part I

Chapter 1: We Have No Control
Chapter 2: Government Regulated Retirement Accounts
Chapter 3: College Costs
Chapter 4: Debt
Chapter 5: Mortgage Debt
Chapter 6: Automobile Loans
Chapter 7: Credit Card Debt

Part II

Chapter 8: Finding The Money
Chapter 9: How To Pay Off Your Home Early
Chapter 10: Self Finance Your Next Auto Loan
Chapter 11: College Savings
Chapter 12: Saving For Retirement
Chapter 13: Another Income Protection Solution
Chapter 14: In Retirement
Chapter 15: Types Of Cash Value Life Insurance
Chapter 16: Final Thoughts

Introduction:

Well hello there! My name is Derek and I have had this burning desire inside of me to write this. I feel like the information contained in this book will be vital to the financial well being of so many in this great nation of ours.

Make no mistake. We are living in unprecedented times. In fact, they are fascinating and yet can seem a bit scary at the same time. The world is moving super fast, politicians are more polarized than ever before, and we are seeing technology move at a pace that the world has never known.

At the same time, the financial system continues to fail the middle class. The middle class continues to shrink, causing more and more people to struggle financially. When we take into consideration flat wages, rising costs of living, health care, etc. we can begin to understand why middle America is becoming an endangered species.

On top of all of that, we are a consumer driven society. Whenever I flip on the TV, I notice commercial after commercial pushing their products and services on us. What I have also noticed is that there seem to be more commercials than actual shows these days. All I can say is thank goodness for DVR!

My point with the commercials is every time we turn around, we are being asked to buy something. We want to impress others, have the latest & nicest things, feel good, even if at the expense of being financially secure.

There was a Lending Tree commercial [1] several years back. It was about a guy named Stan. He had a four bedroom home with a pool, a brand new car, and belonged to the local golf club. Then, he says, "how do I do it? I'm in debt up to my eyeballs. Somebody please help me." In fact, go to YouTube and see for yourself.

Keep in mind the company that put out this commercial is Lending Tree. In other words, a company that helps people borrow money.

It is time we take a step back from this crazy reality we are living in. Companies are deliberately targeting those not financially educated and it is costing people their financial peace of mind.

Think about it. Today, we can order anything on Amazon and have it delivered within a day or two. We don't even need to get dressed anymore.

Want some ice cream from the local ice cream shop? No problem! UberEats has you covered. Come to think of it, you can get food delivered from just about any restaurant in town, even if that particular restaurant doesn't deliver.

Now, I am not against these conveniences. As a matter of fact, I have embraced them. If we do not embrace certain changes, we will be left behind. I mention them because it is far easier to spend more money than it was even a decade ago. Our technology is progressing at lightning speeds.

On the flip side, changes to how we save and grow our money has also been evolving, and it is not all positive. This is why I am writing this now. It is time that we get back to fundamentals with our money. New government regulated plans are doing us a disservice and we all must adjust swiftly.

Over the course of this simple, yet powerful read, I will explain why these plans are a potential financial time bomb for you as well as provide alternatives that are far safer.

The only thing I ask of you is that you maintain an open mind. We have had commercials and entertainers pound into us how it should be done, yet, one of the biggest concerns of people in or close to retirement is outliving their money. It is true! There are tens of thousands of people who are more afraid of running out of money than they are of dying. Put that into perspective.

It is my hope that this does serve as a wake up call to you, and I would also urge you to share these pages with friends and loved ones. They will thank you dearly for it.

About me:

Let me tell you a little bit about me, my background, and what got me so passionate about helping middle America.

I grew up on Long Island, New York, and lived there until age 22. I don't come from wealth nor do I have any major connections. In fact, at age 19, I was floundering around, living at home, and going nowhere with my life.

It was then that my neighbor, who was working in New York City, suggested I come check out where he worked. I figured what the heck, I'll take a ride into Manhattan. After all, what else was I doing, not to mention, I was constantly seeking a way to move out of my parents house.

I went into the city and got hired. If my memory serves me well, I was being paid $300 a week and had unlimited upside potential. My job, before I was to obtain my Series 7 license, was to cold call business owners and executives.

If you are following me, I was on my way to being a stockbroker. I was very excited, especially after seeing some of the checks the other brokers were taking home.

This company, which shall remain unnamed, was in midtown Manhattan and was founded by some who left a company called Stratton Oakmont. If that does not ring a bell, Stratton Oakmont was the firm run by Jordan Belfort, who the movie Wolf of Wall St.[2] is about.

While I did get my license working here, I also hated what I was doing. I ended up leaving and going to work for a firm on Long Island for several months before realizing this was certainly not what I want to be doing for the rest of my life. Good thing, as most of these firms were eventually shut down, as they were mainly fraudulent.

I decided that I would love to get a job on the New York Stock Exchange(NYSE)[3] shortly after though. I went down there and got hired as a ticket runner, for $5 an hour, as a temp. The goal was to be noticed and picked up by a company.

In June of 1997, I had been running and hustling down there for about 3 months and people were noticing. This was the same month I also got hired by a firm.

I went on to work with this firm until January of 2008. When I mention this to others, most immediately ask if I left because of the economy. Remember, it was 2007-2008, when housing crashed and the economy took a major hit. The stock market dropped about 54% over that time, and millions of people lost their jobs and life savings. [4]

The reality of the NYSE itself was that we were automated out of business. It had zero to do with the economy. The NYSE really made the push for automation after September 11, 2001. This was one of the darkest days in our nation's history, and certainly the worst day of my life.

You see, the NYSE was always a potential terrorist target and so the less people down there, the better off it would be. I think there were many other reasons, but that's a whole other conversation.

So, why do I tell you all of this? What does this have to do with helping you plan for your future? It has everything to do with it. It was because of automation that I quickly realized just how unprepared I was for the next chapter of my life. It was automation, coupled with the Great Recession, that helped mold my philosophies to make sure, people like you and me, can be set up to weather almost any financial storm.

You see, I had clients that were mutual and hedge funds, high net worth individuals, as well as brokerage companies. I was on top of the world, until I wasn't.

When our industry turned to automation, I was forced to find a new career. At first I did pretty well.

I worked for a remodeling company doing in home sales and design for kitchens and bathrooms.

Ultimately I wanted to get back into financial services. It was just something I always had a passion for and I felt such a strong desire to restart my career there.

I also wanted to understand retirement plans more. Unfortunately, when I left Wall St., I had a 401(k), 529 plans for my girls, and other savings. First, we tapped into savings, as I was just never earning the kind of money I did while down on the NYSE.

Once the savings were gone, we then took a distribution on the girls 529 plans. I had one of the plans on my oldest for about four years. The good and bad news about the 529 plans was this.

Good news was we didn't have to pay any IRS penalties. The bad news was the account never earned a dime. We didn't totally understand these types of plans, and I worked on Wall St., so we never took advantage of state tax credits. If we had, we would have owed that money back.

With my 401(k), which had since been rolled into an IRA, or Individual Retirement Account, was another story. When we began taking distributions, out of financial desperation by the way, not only did we have to pay taxes on every penny we took, but we were also faced with an IRS penalty of 10%.

This angered us greatly and I then became determined, to not only understand how these plans really work, but to share with everybody I came into contact with. These government regulated plans can be super confusing and I am on a mission to help you understand how they really work.

The rest of this book will be dedicated to helping you understand what is going on in our country, how it relates to your pocket, and what you can do to maximize your savings and help you become financially free.

Part I will be dedicated to helping you understand money, debt, and all the pitfalls. It is laid out in a way that is simple, yet effective and super easy to understand. It may also get you angry, but that's okay, as Part II will provide solutions and answers for you. Enjoy!

Part I

Chapter 1

We Have No Control

When I say we have no control, I am not attempting to issue some blanket statement. There are plenty of things in life that we control, or at least have the ability to control.

For instance, off the top of my head, I can control my attitude toward others. We all have this ability, not that we exercise it regularly. We can control the foods we eat, the exercise, or lack thereof we do, the books we read, the television we watch, and so on. If you took the we have control statement as a one size fits all, you shouldn't.

Now let's dive into what we cannot control. The number one thing that pops into my head are the stock markets. Now, the markets, as of this writing, are at all time highs. With that said, we never know what tomorrow
may bring.

Allow me to share a quick story with you, back when I worked on the NYSE in New York City. It was a Tuesday morning, quite a beautiful day, and it was just another day of heading into work. Erin, my future wife, and I exercised that morning before work.

We briefly chatted after and I went into the Stock Exchange building while she mentioned going to the World Trade Center to get stuff for her hair. For those of you who are not familiar, the World Trade Center had a nice mall inside.

While down on the trading floor, I was chatting with a client out in California, as we had time before the Exchange opened for business. While on the phone, one of the brokers came running into the booth yelling,"a plane just hit the Twin Towers!" The World Trade Center was often referred to as the Twin Towers as the two buildings looked almost identical.

Not thinking much of it, and actually feeling bad for the person(s) who misguided their small plane into the building, we suddenly ducked moments later. The next plane had roared over us before crashing into the other tower. It was at this point we knew it was not an accident involving a small plane, but rather an attack with jet airliners.

I'll never forget my friend and co-worker looking at me wide-eyed and saying,"Yo Nellie! Get your shit! We are leaving!" Even though this was about 19 years ago now, his words and tone of voice still ring in my head as if it were yesterday. Oh, yes, Nellie was my nickname down there.

My future wife was working on the American Stock Exchange, a few blocks from us, and even closer to the Trade Center. I took a walk over there to see if she was okay, and to get her out of there.

As I walked, I could see the two towering sky-scrapers burning. It was something out of a movie. This is also a sight in my mind that will be burned in for as long as I live.

When I got to the American Exchange, I was confronted by security. I showed my NYSE badge and they allowed me to enter the lobby.
Erin came out and told me that Dick Grasso[5], then Chairman of the NYSE, had said the markets would have a delayed opening.

I said, "Delayed!", in disbelief. Then I asked if she had seen what was going on out there and that it looked like a war zone. With that said, she convinced me it would be fine and I should head back.

We had an office in Hanover Square, which was right about the southern tip of Manhattan, and only about a half mile walk for me.

If you know anything about New York City life, it just doesn't make sense to have a car. Walking, cabs, and subways are life. Oh, and if you are wondering, I don't miss the hustle and bustle of the city.

Just as I got to the office, which was on the 22nd floor, the news reported that the first tower had collapsed. Within a minute, it completely engulfed our building and we were smothered in total darkness.

This is when I started to lose it. Has the building collapsed onto the American Stock Exchange? Yes, it was that close. Is Erin Okay? Will I ever see her again? I am sure you could imagine the crazy thoughts and emotions running through my head. It was fear, anxiety, anger, and hopelessness all wrapped into one moment.

It was at this time that cell phone service was cut off. Now that our flip phones didn't work, we could not confirm if others were okay.

As the air cleared up, I gathered my thoughts and was hoping for a miracle. Then suddenly another rumble, and then darkness over us once again. The second tower had come down. All those crazy thoughts and emotions came right back.

Eventually, the air did clear, and at about 11am, cell service was restored. I got a call from Erin. It was like the weight of the world had just been taken off me. She was okay. They bussed them out of there prior to the first building coming down.

I asked where she was and she said the New York

Public Library[6]. This was going to be a hike, but I didn't care. I was more than happy to take that walk. I took off my dress shirt and soaked it in water. Then I wrapped it around my nose and mouth so I would limit the toxins I was breathing in.

Why do I tell you this story and what does it have to do with saving money and improving your financial situation? I tell you this because this was a day that we had no control over. Who in the world could have anticipated a group of highly trained terrorists would have hijacked jetliners full of innocent people and use them as missiles?

This event is what is known as a Black Swan event. The definition of Black Swan is: an unpredictable or unforeseen event, typically one with extreme consequences. These events can occur at any time and with little or no warning.

Another example of a Black Swan event is Hurricane Katrina back in 2005. While meteorologists and news people tracked the storm, they had no idea of the destruction it would cause. Did you know New Orleans never really fully recovered and they still cannot guarantee the levies would withstand another storm like that?

It is events like these that could wreak havoc on markets and the economy. What would it mean to you if your retirement portfolio dropped 20, 30, or even 50%? What if your savings took a massive hit when you were about to retire?

Could you imagine working your entire life, diligently saving in your 401(k), only to have all of your retirement dreams shattered because of a market collapse?

You don't think it is possible? Find some people who were affected by the housing market crash, which almost brought our whole economy to the brink. Ask them what they did.

Now fortunately, markets not only bounced back, but for those who had the time to ride it out, the markets took off like a rocket ship! We continue to make all time highs, as of January of 2020.

What if the markets dropped and never recovered though? What if your portfolio took a 40% hit and just stayed there? How would that affect your plans? To put things into perspective, if you saved $700,000 and the market dropped 40%, you would now have $420,000. This would have a major impact on retirement income.

If you don't think it is possible, look at Japan. In the 1980's all we heard about was the high flying economy of Japan. They were investing all over the United States, had the hottest economy and stock market, and were considered, by many, the wealthiest people on Earth.

What they also lived in were long term, record low interest rates, property and public company valuations that more than tripled in value, speculation, and a soaring stock market. Then, it all came tumbling down. Does any of this sound familiar?

You see, once they realized there was a bubble, they raised interest rates in an effort to curb all the speculation that was happening. This caused their stock market to collapse and created a debt crisis.

On January 4, 1990, Japan's stock market, known as the Nikkei 225, opened at 38,921. By December 5, 1990, it dropped to 21,902. That is a 43% drop within a year. Right now, as I write this, it is at 23,850. It never made a recovery.[7]

I am not predicting nor am I forecasting the same for the United States, so please do not misconstrue why I am writing this. All I am saying is that it could happen and that a lot of what is going on here today sounds eerily familiar to what happened in Japan decades ago.

I just feel like we must take control of our own financial lives and grow our money safely, so that this type of risk could never ruin us financially. It is all about taking back control, and when it comes to your finances, control is a powerful thing.

Chapter 2

Government Regulated
Retirement Accounts

Government sure enjoys dipping their hands in our pockets and having control, and I am here to tell you, your retirement account is no different. I like to compare our government to a casino, which makes you the one sitting at the blackjack table. Sure, people win when they gamble, but you know who else wins? The house. In fact, the house always wins.

The larger problem with retirement accounts is that there is more than one house winning, while you take 100% of the risk and they have none.

Now, when I speak of Government regulated retirement accounts, several of these plans fall into this category including: 401(k), IRA, 403(b), 457 plans, and others. For the sake of understanding, I am going to focus on the 401(k), as it is the most widely used plan.

Let us begin with a brief history on how the 401(k) was born. In 1978, Congress made some changes to the tax code. The purpose was to allow company bonuses and stock options to get tax deferral. In other words, get compensated today and pay taxes on that compensation at a future date. Very similar to how most retirement plans, including the 401(k) are structured.

In 1980, Ted Benna, also known as the father of the 401(k), figured out how to use this tax code change and create a savings plan for employees. Although it was not popular at first, he was able to get the IRS to change some rules in 1981 so that the 401(k) could be funded through employee salary deductions.

Within a few short years, nearly half of large companies were offering 401(k) plans to their employees. As of this writing, there are over $5 trillion in 401(k) plans!

Ted Benna, the father of the 401(k), is on record saying that he created a monster. He also has stated that it was never meant to be someone's sole source of retirement savings and that changes must be made.

This is where the IRS & Wall St., the house, come back into the picture. Whether the markets are up or down, these two players get paid. The 401(k) is literally one of the very few things people will buy into without knowing the risks, costs, or future implications. That's exactly why advocates, such as myself, need to step up and alert the public.

If you participate in your company's 401(k) plan,

have you ever looked into what the costs are? They do a fantastic job of burying the costs so it is not easy to locate. What if I told you that you were paying 2-3% every year? What is this costing you over the long term?

Let's simplify things a bit. If the market is up 5%, you earn 2-3%. If the market is up 10%, you earn 7-8%. Now, if the market is down 5%, you are down 7-8% and if the market is down 10%, well, you lose 12-13%.

So whom or where do these fees go? Your plan provider and to the funds themselves that you pick. In other words, whether you earn money or lose money on any given year, Wall St. gets paid.

So, what about the other part of the house I mentioned, the Internal Revenue Service, or IRS? The IRS has set it up so they are guaranteed revenue at a later date.

You see, when investing our hard earned dollars into a retirement plan, such as a 401(k), we are told that we will be saving money in taxes, as they are deferred. What about the opposite?

What if, by delaying paying our taxes until a future date, we are actually compounding our future tax bill? Think about it. At the time of this writing, federal taxes are historically low.

For example, for a couple earning $50,000, that would ultimately put them into a 22% tax bracket for some of those earnings. If this was the year 1989, any money earned over $30,950 for a married couple would be taxed at 28%.

If you go even further back, let's say 1975 since that's my birth year, anything earned over $28,000 for a married couple would have been taxed at 39%! Imagine earning $50,000 and only keeping about half.

I constantly hear politicians speaking about higher taxes. I have to believe it is only a matter of time before we are paying more in federal taxes.

So, I ask, would you rather pay taxes now, when they are historically low, or would you rather wait until they are potentially much higher?

What about state tax that most have to pay? Let's face it, both state and federal governments are broke and operate in the red. If any of us attempted to run a real business like this, we wouldn't last 6 months before shutting down.

With that said, the federal government continues to print money, further devaluing the dollar. The states however, cannot print money. What are they to do?

States will often issue bonds to cover immediate obligations, such as pensions. What are bonds exactly? They are debt instruments. They borrow money from investors and pay them interest over a period of time.

Yes, you read that correctly. States are taking on debt to pay debt and it is happening on a national scale. I equate it to using a credit card to pay your utility bills. Eventually, the system will implode.[8]

As federal and state governments grow more desperate to collect money, they may eventually turn to retirement accounts. Make no mistake, many people with pensions are already being affected and it won't be long before they begin to raise taxes, reduce benefits, and yes, even find a way to further tax retirement plans.

We have heard whispers of a distribution tax. When a retirement account owner takes a distribution, or income, from their account, they are required to pay federal and other applicable taxes.

Distributions are treated in the same manner as income. A distribution tax would be an additional fee on top of all the other income taxes you will be paying, further reducing your net income.

This is assuming, of course, that you are over the age of 59 ½. If you are under 59 ½ and take a distribution, then on top of the taxes you pay, the IRS will impose a 10% penalty for early distributions.

This limits access to your money. Conceptually, I get it. We don't want people dipping into their nest eggs for frivolous purchases.

In reality, we may require access to that money if we suffer a job loss, or would like to utilize the money elsewhere.

I feel that a Roth 401(k) or IRA would be a better option for most. These retirement vehicles will allow a person to grow retirement savings and have a tax free income source in retirement.

Now, when it comes to Roth accounts, there are a different set of rules that apply. The most attractive part about Roth accounts is that they are tax free upon distribution.

One of the rules, however, is that the account must be in force for a minimum of 5 years in order to qualify for the tax free status. Once 5 years have passed, all distributions are 100% tax free, and this includes the growth.

Another benefit to having a Roth account is there are no required minimum distributions, or RMDs. This is a guideline established by our government that forces retirement account owners to take distributions every year, beginning at age 72, or be faced with a 50% penalty. During this writing, Roth accounts have no RMDs.

You may be wondering why one would potentially be forced to take distributions in a Roth account if they aren't paying taxes on that money.

The answer is this. If we take distributions from Roth accounts, especially if we don't need the income, won't people place those funds into an interest bearing account?

Won't the earnings in those accounts most likely be taxable? Most taxable investment and savings vehicles are shorter term, so this would give the government more tax revenue.

What you would run into, whether a traditional retirement account or a Roth, is that it is a government regulated plan. To me, this means a couple of things. For one, the government can, and does, change the rules whenever they so please.

In this environment, where the government continues to pile on the debt and print money, who is to say that Roth accounts will be tax free forever? While they may not require income tax to be paid, they could conceptually charge a distribution tax.

If and when they do decide to add a distribution tax, won't the government also require the money be taken out, just like a traditional retirement account? After all, they need the revenue to cover the outrageous spending.

Another major concern is Social Security. We all contribute to Social Security for years and years and expect to have a monthly income when we reach retirement age.

I am currently 45 years old and the full retirement age for collecting Social Security benefits is expected to be at least 67 years old. I am anticipating full retirement age, when I actually get into my 60's, could be 70 or older.

In addition, the way things are going, between healthcare costs and many of the entitlements, Social Security may eventually only be available to those who qualify. What if those qualifications were similar to food stamps, medicaid, and other programs?

What I mean is simply, in order to receive Social Security benefits, which you contributed to, you could only have a certain amount of assets. The less assets we have, the more likely we would be to qualify for Social Security benefits.

Now, even if you have a Roth account and it remains tax free, since this is a government regulated account, won't this be an asset they know about? Could this not potentially disqualify you from collecting on a program you spent decades contributing to?

I am not telling you all of this to pump fear into you and scare you. I want you to be educated and understand what is happening and what the future may hold for us. Wall St. and other regulators want us in the dark so they can continue their business as usual.

I want you to be educated so that you have the knowledge and know how to do what's best for you and your family, rather than lining the pockets of Wall St. and regulators.

Chapter 3

College Costs

Many of our children will be attending some sort of college or university. With what we know about college debt, and all the talk we hear, I am sure we would love if our children graduated with zero student loan debt.

As it stands today, student loan debt is over $1.6 Trillion.[9]

College costs are astronomical, and on average, rise about 8% annually. The current average cost for a four year degree, in state, public college, is $21,477 a year. This means that in four years, that four year degree would cost $85,788.

In ten years, this same scenario will cost $46,302 per year and $208,644 for four years. This makes it nearly impossible for most of our children to graduate debt free.

How can someone graduate without a ton of debt that will take years to pay off? If you didn't already know this, now you will. If the person whose student loan debt their name is in, declares bankruptcy, the student loan does not go away. It is very unforgiving.

With that said, there are things we can do to lower these costs. Many of us may qualify for financial aid. There are many different forms of financial aid, some of which do not have to be paid back while other forms do.

For example, a student can be awarded a scholarship. Scholarships come in many forms and even if your child isn't a superstar athlete or straight A student, they may qualify for some sort of scholarship.

To give you an idea, a student could receive a scholarship for being creative, doing community service, or even winning a scholarship contest. These types of financial aid do not have to be repaid, and will reduce the overall costs.

There are other forms of aid, such as Pell Grants,[10] that do not have to be repaid. Being awarded a Pell Grant and how much would depend on a few factors:

- Full time or part time student
- Financial need
- Cost of College or University

There are many other grants and scholarships, which do not need to be paid back, but you must apply. The way you would do this is by filling out an application. This application is called Free Application for Federal Student Aid(FAFSA).

Other forms of financial aid do need to be paid back. There are loans available to people that have an extraordinary financial need.

These loans are called Perkins loans and will have a lower interest rate than a standard student loan. A standard student loan varies, but could have an interest rate, as of today, as high as 7% whereas a Perkins loan may have an interest rate of 5%.

This book is not intended to be a college financial aid and loans course, so please make sure you do your homework when it comes time for your child to apply.

Chapter 4

Debt

One of the major issues we face, both as a nation and as households, is too much debt. I am going to touch on the nation's debt issues, and then we will dive into how personal debts are affecting households all across the country.

I would highly recommend that you do not skip this section. Even if you are completely debt free, you can better understand how to stay out of financial trouble as well as educate others. It is especially important that our children learn this sooner rather than later as well.

As a nation, we are in big trouble financially. It doesn't matter if you are a Democrat, Republican, or independent. There is a four letter word no politician can dance around, though they do a great job at pretending. That four letter word is MATH.

As of this writing, the United States, arguably the richest country in the history of the world, has a national debt of over $23 trillion! According to Truth in Accounting, the real debt is over $121 trillion.[11] How is this so?

The published national debt does not include unfunded Social Security or Medicare promises, nor the other liabilities, which are listed in the Financial Report of the U.S. Government.

I want you to understand something very important. This debt will not only never be paid back, it is expected to get much, much worse.

To put that $121 trillion into perspective, this is a $792,000 burden on every tax payer. The majority of people in this country don't have that kind of money for retirement, let alone paying down the debt.

As we continue down this road, debts will continue to rise. Every day for about the next decade, there are roughly 10,000 people turning 65. Doesn't this mean Social Security and Medicare costs will continue to rise?

Aren't people living longer? We could be looking at a published national debt of $50 trillion or more within a decade. This could put the real debt to around $250 trillion.

How will the government sustain? How will they create more revenue? These are the questions that never seem to get answered. Won't they have to raise taxes? We have seen nations become completely stagnant when governments attempt to tax themselves out of trouble.

There are so many ways we could be hit with taxes. Off the bat, we all think of income tax. We are at historically low levels when it comes to the federal taxation of our paychecks. It was not always this way though, and it will not always be so. How could it?

Now, I understand inflation, but for the purpose of simplicity, let's see what nominal tax rates have been historically for a married couple earning $40,000.

Year	Earning	Tax Rate
2019	$40,000	12%
2009	$40,000	15%
1999	$40,000	15%
1989	$40,000	28%
1979	$40,000	43%
1969	$40,000	48%
1959	$40,000	56%

Again, I totally understand inflation, and there were

fewer people earning $40,000 in 1959 than there were in 2019. Also note that not every dollar earned is taxed at this rate, but rather the dollars earned put one into this tax bracket. This is an ultra simple example, and is meant just for understanding.

With an aging population, the War on Terror, other threats to interests around the world, rising health-care costs, etc., won't the Government have to spend more and more money as time goes on? Ask yourself again. Where will they get the money? From people who have it or people who don't have any?

Isn't it true that if you have a Government regulated plan, that they know exactly what you have in your accounts? Does this mean you will be taxed more and offered less? Isn't it possible that Social Security only goes to those who have no assets, even though everyone is required to pay into it?

I am not trying to be redundant but rather drive home the point that taxes are poised to rise. We have multiple politicians who don't even hide the fact that they want to raise taxes. It is going to happen.

So, I ask. Would you rather pay taxes today, when they are historically low, or would you prefer to roll the dice and defer them to later? Tax risk is a huge risk in my opinion, but it doesn't have to be.

With that said, if you continue to contribute funds to your 401(k) or IRA, this is a risk you are assuming. Also, because you are reading this, you are now well aware of this wealth time bomb.

Okay, now that we have discussed how dysfunctional the government is, let us shift our attention to the consumer, or better known as you and I.

We are a consumer driven society. What this means is that our economy thrives on people like you and I, when we spend money. The more we are spending, the higher the consumer confidence indicators rise(yes this is a real measure), and the better the economy appears to be doing.

Here is the problem though. Prices have gone way up over the past 20 years, yet wages remain relatively flat. I attribute this as the main reason families cannot ever seem to get ahead. Look at the average family today, and it might be very similar to your situation.

Jim and Stephanie have been married for 9 years. They have 2 children, ages 6 and 3, own two vehicles, and have a home in a typical suburban neighborhood. They are in love and get along great. Both their kids are very pleasant, and on the surface, life appears to be working out just fine for them.

The reality tells another story though. Jim and

Stephanie both work full time. He is a manager and she is an assistant. Together, they earn about $80,000 a year.

If we were to take all things into consideration, let us assume that, after taxes, they keep $64,000 or $5,333.33 per month. So far, it still doesn't sound too bad for a family. Where they, and most others, get caught up in the expense column. Below is a table to illustrate how quickly their money disappears:

Monthly Expenses	Amount	Money Left
Mortgage(Including taxes)*	$1,579.20	$3,754.13
2 Vehicles**	$920.83	$2,833.30
Auto Insurance	$275.00	$2,558.30
Day Care	$600	$1,958.30
Groceries	$750	$1,208.30
Cell Phones	$150	$1,058.30
Cable/WIFI	$80	$978.30
Electric Bill	$150	$828.30

Water Bill	$50	$778.30
Term Insurance for Each of Them	$125	$653.30
Netflix	$12.99	$640.31
Gas for Vehicles	$150	$490.31
Misc dinners, pizza, etc	$100	$390.31

*Assumes a $175,000 mortgage and $3,500 in property taxes, 30 year loan, 4.50% interest rate
**Financed vehicles $50,000 total, 5 year loan, 4% interest

By looking at that expense table, you can clearly see there isn't much money left over. What if they had some sort of emergency? Does one of their employers pay for 100% of their health insurance? What about $100 for pizza and a couple of date nights?

I don't know about you, but I have three kids and every time we order pizza, it is between $35-$50! Granted, we only do this about twice per month on average, but you get the point, or at least I hope you do.

What about saving for retirement? Not even listed up there. How could they though? Let's break this down for a moment. If they were to save, let's say $200 of the $390 left over, that would be $2,400 a year. If they saved that for 25 years, they would have saved $60,000.

Of course, this would be in an IRA or 401(k), so let's give this a compounding growth of 5%. Not likely, but it would be amazing if possible.
Based on a 5% compounding growth, they would have $114,545 in 25 years. However, like they say on those infomercials, but wait! There's more!

If you recall what you read on the Government regulated plans, wouldn't every dollar be taxed? The answer is yes! Assuming taxes didn't go up by retirement, after taxes, they would be left with $91,636. This is less than 1.5x their take home today.

How long will this money last them? What about inflation and cost of living? This money wouldn't last them but a year. Then what will they do? Well, they will have Medicare for insurance and Social Security as income right?

Is Social Security enough to live on? I've come across many who solely depend on Social Security, and I have got to tell you, they are struggling. This is not where any of us want to end up.

This is also a scenario that would cause a family to eventually turn to credit cards, the kiss of financial death in my mind. I know because many years ago, I fell into this trap. This is another reason why I am so passionate today about helping people escape the debt trap and maximize savings.

Chapter 5

Mortgage Debt

If you are anything like me, when you were younger, you aspired to own your first home. After all, this is part of the American dream right? Funny thing is, not too long after being in our first home, we wondered if we could set up a plan of attack to pay the mortgage early.

For most, especially with first home, we put little or nothing down. The main reason is the median home prices in the past twenty years, have risen over $152,000! That in itself could be a mortgage.

Now, it's not the rising home prices that are the issue, but rather wages not keeping pace. During this same period(2000-2020), the median income is up just over $3,200.[12] Let's put this into perspective, when it comes to purchasing a home.

In the year 2000, if you had, let's say $10,000 saved for a home, you could get a home, on average, for about $161,000. Keeping things simple, you would borrow $151,000 over 30 years and at 5% interest, your payment would be $810, not including insurance or taxes.

Today, if you were to purchase the same exact

home, and with the same scenario, you would have to borrow $303,000. Now, your monthly payment, before taxes and insurance, would be $1,884.

No wonder Middle America cannot seem to get ahead. This payment is more than double, and yet, incomes have barely risen.

The next question is, what is this mortgage ultimately costing you? As you know, there is a price to pay for anything and everything.

The math is very simple here. If you take the $1,884 and multiply it by the 30 years, you get your total cost. In other words, your $313,000 home will end up costing you $678,240!

This number is an astounding $375,240 above what you paid in this particular scenario. That is a lot of interest to pay the lender. Keep in mind that interest rates are low today as well. Will they be at these levels in a decade? Who knows?

People will generally have three reactions when I show them this:

- It is ridiculous for me to have to pay that much interest
- I won't be in this home for 30 years
- I have to live somewhere

While it may seem crazy to pay the lender that

much interest back, there are not too many people who can just pay cash for their home. In addition, even if you could, does it always make financial sense to fork over that kind of money? In other words, what is the opportunity cost? We will dive into this in part II.

Very true, most people will not own just one home or have a single mortgage over a 30 year period. We move, upgrade, downsize, refinance, etc. With that said, we will almost always still maintain a mortgage. Very few of us ever live in a mortgage free home, though most people wish they were.

We all have to live somewhere. Is owning a home better than renting one? Typically yes, in my opinion. Unless your work calls for extensive travel, and you are constantly on the move, it usually makes sense to own a home.

The number one advantage to owning vs renting is that you know what your payment will be. That remains fixed for the entire length of that particular mortgage. Now, taxes, association dues, and other expenses rise, but the mortgage payment itself remains level.

Rents rise over time. In fact, if you have ever rented one place over a few years, you will notice that, most of the time, your rent will rise upon each renewal. Rents go up over time, just like any other expense.

With all of that said, I am not against having a mortgage. I don't buy into the whole be mortgage free no matter what concept. There are many ways to put your money to work for you, your home just isn't one of those ways.

Chapter 6

Automobile Loans

Something else that is rarely paid for up front are the vehicles we drive. Like home prices, the cost of an automobile has also soared. If you look back to the year 2000, the average vehicle was just over $22,000. The average price today is over $38,000! This is a $16,000 increase.

One of the main catalysts for rising prices is technology. Many of us are essentially driving computers. There are also a ton of SUVs on the road, which certainly brings up the average cost.

Are you aware that, as of this writing, auto loan debt is over $1.2 Trillion! On top of that, because of rising costs of vehicles, people are taking out longer term loans in an effort to lower the payment. What people don't understand is this lower payment is costing big time!

Allow me to show you what I mean in this chart:

Monthly Payment

Amount Borrowed	Interest Rate	60 Months	72 Months	84 Months
$25,000	5%	$472	$403	$353
$35,000	5%	$661	$564	$495
$45,000	5%	$849	$725	$636

Let's look at the $35,000 loan so you can understand. On a 60 month loan, your payment would be $661 per month. You will pay a total of $39,660 or $4,660 in interest.

When you extend this loan to 6 or 7 years to lower your payments, it actually becomes more expensive.

A 72 month loan will cost you $40,608 or $5,608 in interest and an 84 month loan will cost $41,580 or $6,580 in interest.

The true interest rate on the 72 month loan, for example, is not 5%, but rather 16%. How is this possible you ask? The answer, Annual Percentage Rate, or APR.

Notice on these loans, as you pay them down, your payment remains the same. This is where they get you. It is simple math. I divide the amount borrowed into the interest paid to get my answer. This is how you calculate the real interest rate, and the longer the term, the higher the rate. This would give an 84 month loan, at 5%, a real interest rate of

18.8%!

Right now, you may be scratching your head, feeling perplexed, or even angry, but again, this book is meant to be a financial awakening. The sooner we understand all of this, the better chance of financial success we will have in the long run. Remember, all of the solutions will be discussed in part II.

Chapter 7

Credit Card Debt

Credit card debt in this country is an astronomical $1.1 Trillion and shows no sign of slowing down.[13] How much interest is being paid to credit card companies? Imagine if we could shift from paying this interest to actually earning interest.

Currently, the average household is holding just under $8,400 in credit card debt and the average interest rate on that debt is 17.30%. When it comes to credit cards, most of us are paying the minimum that is due.

If your minimum is $336 per month(4% of balance), then it will take 151 months or 12.58 years to pay back. The real kicker is this debt will end up costing $4,616 in interest alone. This is why the banks and lenders continue to make fortunes while Middle America struggles to get by.

Consumer debt is one of the main reasons we struggle to save money. We literally finance everything. We finance our cars, homes, and even cell phones. I am not here saying it is all bad, but for so many, we tend to overextend ourselves to the brink of financial ruin.

Even though you may qualify for a loan, this doesn't mean you may not be stretching yourself a bit too thin. Sure, as long as all is going well, status quo, you earn enough to continue your lifestyle.

What happens if you all of a sudden need a new refrigerator? What if your boiler dies on you? Ever think what your life would look like if you, all of a sudden, had a stroke and required 9 months of rehabilitation?

What would you do? Being that so many are check to check, we would have to take out more debt by either financing a project or swiping the old Visa card.

This is a financial disaster in the making. Are you prepared to overcome an unexpected financial burden? If you needed access to funds tomorrow, how much could you get?

These kinds of questions force you to look at, not only the reality of your situation, but also the what ifs. Most of us would rather ignore, pretend everything is fine, and hope for the best. In reality, people are scared. People lose sleep over the what ifs. Take inventory by asking these questions listed below:

- What if my roof needs replacement?
- What would happen if I get injured and can't

work for 6+ months?
- Could we stay in our home if my income stopped?
- What if I become critically ill or suffered a stroke?
- What would we do if I lost my job?
- If I passed away today, what would my family do?

These are very thought provoking questions and you should not hide from them. If you face them head on, then plans can be developed to maximize your chances for financial success. The second part of this book will be dedicated to solutions and financial peace of mind.

Part I I

Chapter 8

Finding The Money

The first step to getting out of debt, having more money on a monthly basis, and maximizing your savings, is to find the money. What do I mean by finding the money?

Am I talking about finding a few quarters among the crumbs under the sofa cushions? Maybe you forgot about the thousands of dollars you buried in your mattress a few years back. Wouldn't that be a pleasant surprise. That's not what I am referring to though.

What I am talking about is moving things around to free up money without having to ask for a raise or take on another job.

Whenever I meet with a potential client, whether in person or over the phone, we always figure out a way to put more dollars in their pockets every month. Allow me to give you a quick example.

I recently had a meeting with Tom. Tom had actually just requested information about getting his mortgage protected. Tom had a nice home, about 3,000 square feet, nice cars in the driveway, and on the surface, looked like he was doing really well.

Then I began asking some questions that really had him thinking and wondering what he should do. I learned that Tom was earning $110,000 a year, had a 401(k), but also had a ton of bills.

He explained that he was contributing $600 a month to his 401(k) plan. Over the next 15 years, he will contribute $108,000, and in twenty, contribute a total of $144,000.

He was also contributing to several credit cards. Yes contributing. Making high interest payments to credit card companies, to the tune of $800 a month. This doesn't even include the auto loans, which brought it up to over $1,000 every month.

Our main focus was getting rid of those cards. This is such a typical scenario and I see it all the time. Tom is putting $600 a month into his 401(k), hoping to earn 7%, while paying double digit interest to the credit card companies. This is a major reason so many people struggle to get ahead.

What I recommended he do in this situation was to immediately cease paying into his retirement plan and redirect those funds to wipe out the credit cards. From there, I helped him structure the right way to pay down the cards to minimize his interest paid. I am just so happy he listened.

During our initial conversation, I also discovered he was having the maximum taxes taken out of each paycheck, or filing Single 0. Keep in mind he is married and has two children. Tom got a decent refund every year so he was happy with that.

What I did next was to explain that the refund he gets was his money all along. He was essentially loaning the money to the IRS, interest free, and that money was earning zero. To put another way, the money the IRS is holding earns you no money, then credit cards are used because there isn't enough net income, forcing you to pay high interest rates.

When money earns zero, it loses value due to rising costs and inflation. A dollar today may only be worth $.96 this time next year. It was then he got it. I had him change his dependents to married 4. He was comfortable with that.

That would put a few extra hundred dollars back in his pocket every month. This way, he could avoid using credit cards all together as he paid them down. The reason he was using them in the first place was because sometimes there just wasn't enough money in the account.

Once the money is found, paying down credit cards and other debt becomes easy. Just like with Tom, the reason he was falling deeper into the debt trap was because of not enough cash flow. Whether someone earns $40,000 a year or $140,000, it is very easy to slip into this trap.

What we do, as advisers, is take a look from the outside, with no emotion, and help you devise a plan to eliminate that debt as fast as possible. Often times, it is a second pair of eyes that might just see things a little differently than you. Let us be those eyes.

Chapter 9

How To Pay Off Your Home Early

In this section, we discuss options for paying off the home early. When we were younger, most of us rented an apartment or condo. Why though? Mainly because we were just getting going and we just did not have the ability to put a down payment and qualify for a mortgage.

Then, it happened! You bought your first home. It was exhilarating and scary all at the same time. You did it! You are officially a homeowner.

Soon after owning your home, whether it be a year or even 5 years down the road, you start exploring ways to pay down the mortgage sooner so you can eliminate that bill.

Isn't it funny how our mindset changes when it comes to home ownership? It's not that we would rather rent, but that we don't want that monthly payment any longer. The beauty of home ownership versus renting is that in time, you can actually eliminate that bill.

Plus, when you are renting, not only will those payments never stop, but they cost more over time, and you never have anything to show for it, with the exception of a bunch of bills. If you recall, all of that interest you would pay on top of what you borrowed, I hope you can understand why you may want to pay the mortgage off early.

With that said, what is the best way to pay down your mortgage? There are several ways to do it, and I don't know what's best for you. Allow me to discuss the three most common ways and let you make that decision for yourself.

The first way would be to send extra payments over the course of the year to reduce the time of the mortgage. If you have the extra funds to do this, you could knock off 5-10 years off a 30 year mortgage. This would save you thousands in interest payments, not to mention kissing that payment goodbye.

Let me give you an example. If you had a 30 year mortgage for $200,000, at 4.50% interest, your payment would be about $1,013 a month. If you pay this for the next 30 years, you would pay a total of $364,680. This is $164,680 in interest alone!

Now, if you could add $200 a month to your current payment, you would pay the 30 year loan about 10 years early. By doing this, your total payments would now be $303,120, reducing your total interest paid by $61,560. Ask yourself, how would an extra $61,000 help you with building your nest egg?

The second option would be to get a shorter term mortgage. For example, you could refinance into a 15 or 20 year mortgage. This will lower your interest rates, but also raise your payments.

With all things being equal, this could potentially bring your interest rate down to 3.75% from 4.50% on a 15 year loan. Payments will still be higher, but if you are attempting to pay the mortgage off early, they would be higher anyhow.

Let us take the same $200,000 loan, only this time, we shorten the term to 15 years. At 3.75%, your monthly mortgage payments would be $1,454. Keep in mind, we are still not including insurance, taxes, or any applicable association fees.

There is no escaping these fees, though relocation can sometimes dramatically lower them. That is exactly what happened when we moved from New York to Florida. Property taxes in states like NY, NJ, IL, and others, are astronomically high.

Okay, now that we have our 15 year loan and know our payments, what is the total cost for borrowing this money? On a $200,000 loan, you would pay a total of $261,720. This is now $61,720 in interest. This is much easier to swallow, then if stretching the mortgage out 30 years. The question is, can you pull it off?

Whether you simply accelerate payments or take out a shorter term mortgage, you will ultimately save thousands upon thousands of dollars in interest.

If I was forced to pick one of these options personally, I would go with sending extra payments. The reason behind it is it is more flexible. What if you had an emergency expense at some point and needed the extra money? If you are in a 15 year loan, then that payment is due.

On the flip side, if you remain in a 30 year mortgage and are making extra payments, when a financial emergency arises, and it will, you can simply make the required payment and have the extra dollars you previously allocated for the extra payments.

If there was a downside to making the extra payments as compared to a fixed required amount, I would say you have to remain disciplined. That's where we come in though. We help so many people find money by shifting debt, getting rid of unnecessary expenses, etc, that it becomes much easier to make these payments month in and month out.

There is no question, that either way you choose, will work. What you should do, however, is consider a few things that life can, and does, throw at us.

The first, as mentioned above, is some sort of financial emergency. These could mean a new central air system, roof replacement, new vehicle, or any number of things we own that could just stop working.

Another very important scenario to consider is what if you were to become critically ill? Are you aware that strokes are the leading cause of disability? In the United States, someone suffers a stroke every 40 seconds.[14]

For most, if someone suffers a stroke, this could mean months of rehabilitation, physical therapy, and healing.

The biggest cause of personal bankruptcies are due to medical expenses. In fact, 66.5% of all personal bankruptcies are a result of medical bills. Here's the kicker. Roughly 75% of those medically induced bankruptcies had some kind of health insurance.

My question to you is how long can you go without a paycheck? Three months, 6 months, a year or more? If your paycheck stopped, what would your family do? Could you continue to stay in your home? Would you foreclose or be forced into bankruptcy?

Keep this in mind. Banks and lenders love to foreclose on homes with more equity. If you had no equity, they would simply have a write off, and probably do everything in their power to get you up to date with payments.

If you have been diligently making the effort to pay your home early and have built up equity, the bank could foreclose on you, sell the home cheaply, and still make a profit. I know, it's heartless, but it's also reality. What we need to do is make sure we are prepared.

With that said, allow me to introduce you to an alternative to pay off your home early. It is possible to do this while maintaining full control, and not sending an extra cent to the lender, until you make that final payment.

Let us redirect those funds into a safe alternative, that allows you full access to your money, should you ever have an emergency. This vehicle is cash value life insurance. Cash value life insurance is probably the greatest financial tool ever created, but ever since the birth of the 401(k), has been bashed by Wall St. Why though? The main reason is Wall St. earns zero money on insurance products.

Now, before I get into how to properly use this savings vehicle, let this be known. Cash value life insurance helps you grow your money safely. You see, if you own mutual funds, your balance can go up, will go down, and no matter what, Wall St. gets paid. In fact, big banks, such as Bank of America, thrive on assets under management.

Assets under management are investments they

hold on your behalf. I am not going to get into microscopic details about this, but I do want you to understand. For every dollar they have, they earn a percent of that. The banks, the fund managers, and the representatives, all get paid. This happens as long as your money is with them. This is also why they will fight tooth and nail should you attempt to leave their firm.

Now let me let you in on a little known fact about the banks, that they do not want you to know about. Banks love life insurance. As a matter of fact, just look at the table below to see how much they own:

Bank	Amount of Cash Value Life Insurance
Wells Fargo	$18 Billion
Bank of America	$22 Billion
JP Morgan Chase	$11 Billion

Banks overall own close to $190 Billion in cash value life insurance. There are many other regional banks, but I figured you would get the point by seeing the above three.[15]

Why would they own so much though? The real answer is simple. It is a tax shelter for the banks and can also offer a tax free source of funds. Banks, among many other industries have learned that they can use the cash value to fund employee benefits on a tax free basis.

The cash value also grows more efficiently than the products they love to sell to Middle America. You know, CDs, mutual funds, etc. Now ask yourself this question. If banks invest their own money into cash value life insurance, why do they sell us CDs and such? It is clear they absolutely do not have our best interests in mind.

To help you understand, when you purchase a CD, you are essentially tying that money up for a period of time. In return, you get a higher interest rate, though still a joke, than you would in a savings account.

The bank sees it as if you are loaning them money and when you give them, let's say $100,000, they can turn around and loan that amount 7-10 times, via mortgages for example. This is called fractional reserve banking. You might be scratching your head a bit, but bear with me.

Now, let's say they loan that money out ten times. On that $1 million, they charge an average of 4.5% interest. With the CD, they might pay you 2.25% on the $100,000, and yet are earning 4.5% on $1 million.

This is what the banks are doing all day every day. They earn billions of dollars every year by taking Mrs. Jones retirement "safe money" and leverage it to earn them more. I don't know about you, but I think it is time for us to take back control!

As a homeowner, what cash value life insurance can do for you is nothing short of astounding. Outside of growing your money with little or no risk, you also solve many potential problems that could occur if you were to become critically ill, disabled, or even pass away unexpectedly.

First and foremost, if you were to pass away and your family lost your income, there is a death benefit paid out. This is something we are all very familiar with.

Assuming you already have at least some life insurance, this new policy is designed specifically to pay off your mortgage early, regardless if you are here or not. In other words, if you die, the mortgage can be paid. If you live, and we all hope you do, there will be sufficient cash value in the policy for you to potentially pay your home 5-15 years early.

Another amazing benefit of using cash value life as a savings vehicle is a feature called waiver of premium. This costs pennies on the dollar and could save you from a financial catastrophe. If you were to ever become fully disabled and could no longer produce an income, waiver of premium would kick in.

What it does is basically pay your premiums to keep your policy going as if you were paying it yourself. Ask yourself this question. What mutual fund, CD, or Wall St. investment would do this?

In addition, you have access to the cash value should the need ever arise. We will get into this more in a bit, but for now, let's say your water heater all of a sudden stopped working. Rather than put it on a credit card, you borrow the money from yourself and pay yourself back.

Once the funds are placed back into your account, it will look like you never even touched it. Why? Well, a properly structured plan will earn money on the entire balance, including the loan, as if you never borrowed it. Sure, the company will charge you interest on the amount you borrowed, but you will earn interest on the entire accumulated value.

This is what the wealthy do, and now I am introducing it to you. I firmly believe we all deserve to have access to savings vehicles that offer us these benefits.

The policy will also be designed, if done correctly, to have the amount of cash value over and beyond what your mortgage balance would be, in 15 years for example.

Chapter 10

Self Finance Your Next Auto Loan

How would you like it if you could be your very own bank? What if you could borrow from yourself when it comes time to get your next vehicle? How incredible would it feel to not have to send payments to a lender and maintain full control? If you are thinking what I'm thinking, you are ready to know how.

If you recall from part I in the part about automobile loans, you read about the real interest being paid, above and beyond what you borrowed. Way too many of us purchase strictly on payments and not on price. Guess what, the automobile industry knows this all too well. This is why they sell on payment.

Now it is time to take back control. Imagine bypassing lenders for the rest of your life? This is another way for your money to circulate and continue to grow, rather than you helping the banks and lenders profit more off your back.

Typically there are a couple of ways we can purchase a vehicle:

- Pay for it outright
- Take a loan

Do you have $25,000-$50,000 sitting around that you want to just hand over for your new vehicle? While this may seem like the most cost effective way to go, it can actually prove to be quite expensive.

You may or may not have heard of a risk called opportunity risk. What this means in this case is that you put your liquid money into something illiquid, and now that cash is gone.

By doing this, you risk losing out on other opportunities. Now when I speak of opportunities, I am referring to potentially earning money with those funds, rather than hand it over for your new automobile.

Also, let us not forget that this vehicle will only depreciate, or go down in value, from the very first day you own it. So, it is really a losing situation for anyone to purchase a new vehicle like this.

What if you had those funds parked in an account earning 3, 5, or even 8% interest? Would you want to remove that growth? Of course not. In fact, I'll bet you would want to put everything you have into something like that. This is where cash value life insurance, once again, comes into play.

One of the biggest wealth destroyers, is interest, if you are paying it. When you take a loan for a new vehicle, isn't that what you are doing? On the flip side, earning interest, would then be a wealth creator. This is exactly what you are doing with your life insurance plan.

What you are reading here is what the wealthy have been doing for well over 100 years now. Wall St. does not want you to know about this. Wall St. wants to manage your money, churn your accounts, and grind every penny they can get out of you. With these strategies, we are keeping money in your pocket, not Wall St. or the lender.

Okay, so you have $40,000 in your cash value life policy. You are in the market for a new Honda, and need about $30,000 to get what you want. Here is what you do.

You request the insurance company send you a check for $30,000 as a loan. They don't ask why, nor do they qualify you through credit checks, income verification, etc. They simply cut you a check.

Since you are taking a loan, you will be charged interest. That interest is 5% for example. Whoa, you shout! They are charging me to borrow my own money? Yes, they are charging you to take a loan, just like when you take equity out of your home, you are charged interest. However, there is a major difference here.

Since you had $40,000 and borrowed $30,000, you will pay interest on the $30,000. Even though you have this loan, when your account earns interest, you will earn interest on the entire $40,000, as if you never took that loan out. This could essentially wash that interest payment out and the earned interest could even be a little higher than what you are paying.

Sound too good to be true? It isn't. In fact, this is exactly how it works. As you are paying yourself back, you earn interest on the entire $40,000, and when you repay yourself back, your account will look like you never even touched it.

How are they able to do that? It is a no risk transaction for an insurance company. When you take a loan, they will lower your death benefit, dollar for dollar, so if you pass away during the time of the loan, your beneficiary will get the death benefit, minus any outstanding loan balance.

I will say that when you borrow from yourself, you want to put this money back, as you are building your nest egg. With that said, if you have an emergency, or happen to miss a payment, no one is going to blow up your phone or send threatening letters that you did not pay. This isn't a lender. You borrowed from yourself remember? Up to you to do the right thing by you and pay it back in a timely fashion.

Chapter 11

College Savings

What is the best way to save for a child's higher education? Before I get into that, allow me to share my own personal philosophy. I am not asking you to agree with me, but it is certainly worth thinking about.

I don't believe the parents or guardians should be saving for a child's higher education until they are max funding their own retirement. Think about it and even read the previous sentence again.

In this great nation of ours, college debt is but just part of our financial woes. We have already discussed automobile debt, credit card debt, and lack of savings overall. Are you aware that in a study conducted just a few years back, a retired person's greatest fear was not death. As a matter of fact, death didn't even make the list.

Concerns ranged from Social Security benefits being reduced or non existent to feeling isolated or alone. Another major concern was declining health and cognitive decline. Yet still, none of these made the top of the list.

The number one concern among retirees is outliving their money.[16] Ask anyone in retirement and they will tell you Social Security is just not enough to live on. We are not saving enough money to feel secure after we retire.

The interesting thing is, many people we talk to have some kind of pension in addition to a retirement account, like a 401(k), that they saved in for years.

This has created my philosophy of don't worry about the kids until you are max funding your own retirement. Remember this key phrase you are about to read. Although not ideal, the kids can always borrow money to continue their education, but you cannot borrow your way through retirement.

So, assuming you are max funding your own future, what is the best way to save for a child's higher education? I can tell you the most popular way. It is a program called a 529 savings plan. Each state has their own plan and there are some tax benefits that go along with them.

Even though you are free to invest in any state's program, typically tax incentives will only benefit those who are investing in the plan within their state of residence. There are some states that will offer a tax benefit to those who do contribute to an out of state plan, but please do your homework before exploring that option.

Now, the money that is already in the account grows tax deferred and withdrawals can be made tax free, provided the funds are used for qualified higher education. But what exactly is a qualified higher education? In other words, if your child pursues a career as an electrician or plumber, their trade school of choice probably will not qualify, under the law.

Now you are probably wondering, what happens to that money? You now have extra savings, which is a great thing, except, you chose the wrong savings vehicle when you opened a 529 savings plan.

If you take withdrawals that are not used for a qualified purpose, then the IRS will hit you with a 10% penalty. You may also be subject to taxes and be required to pay back any tax breaks you received during the time you were saving. Granted, all these fees, taxes, and penalties are only on the gains, but pay them you will nonetheless.

Another option you have with the savings you built within a 529 plan is to transfer it to another child. For example, I have three children. If one of my children, either decides against college or gets some sort of a scholarship, and the funds are not needed, I can transfer those funds to one of my other kids.

On the flip side, if you have one child, your only options are to eat the fees and penalties, or transfer to a niece or nephew. Neither one of these options are very attractive.

To make things more complicated, a 529 savings plan may affect a child's ability to qualify for financial aid. This depends on several factors, but just know that this is a potential issue.

Right now, you are probably thinking about how complicated these plans are, and you would be absolutely correct. I hope you are putting together that pretty much any government savings/retirement program is complicated, and full of rules and restrictions. It is almost as if they are complicated with the purpose of deception.

Now you are curious as to how to save for your children's college education. After all, none of us wants to see our kids graduate with a six figure loan that has to be repaid.

This is where cash value life insurance can play a key role. Think about it. Like a 529 savings plan, the distributions can be taken completely tax free, only it does not have to go toward a higher education.

You heard that correctly! If your child decides to go to a trade school, you can access the money to pay for that. If they get a scholarship, you can use the money as needed, and/or count it toward your own future. How great is that? No 10% IRS penalty, no taxes to be paid, and no paying back previous tax benefits.

Another potential pitfall of the 529 plan is this. What would happen if you opened an account, began contributing, and then died unexpectedly? With cash value life insurance, there is always a tax free benefit paid and that could mean all the money you meant to save, plus more. Again, this money can be used for college, or to help maintain your family's lifestyle.

There are no restrictions on how the money is used, in most cases.
There are two more very important things to consider when deciding to open a college savings plan.

Above, I had mentioned that a 529 plan may affect your child's ability to qualify for financial aid. Although there are a few factors that would influence this, it is something to give serious thought to. Cash value life insurance will never affect financial aid eligibility. Your income might, but not the cash value in the policy.

The other important thing I wanted to mention were gains and losses. Typically in a 529 plan, you would be investing into a fund of some sort. Make no mistake, these are mutual funds, and with mutual funds come fees and market losses. With the life insurance plan, you will not have to be concerned about market losses as you will never be subjected to them.

Chapter 12

Saving For Retirement

You are about to fully discover why a properly structured life insurance plan is the greatest financial tool ever created. You now understand government regulated programs such as the 401(k), IRA, & 529 plan. These vehicles are expensive, complicated, and all come generally with high fees.

When you are saving your hard earned money in these types of accounts, you are always at risk of losing money. At any given time, you could suffer major losses when invested in stocks, mutual funds, or anything that is market correlated.

While you could weather a stock market downturn early in your savings, having similar losses closer to retirement could prove to be devastating. If a 35 year old has been putting money into his company sponsored 401(k), and the stock market drops 20%, he may be down $6,000, assuming there is $30,000 in there.

Later on in life, if that account has grown to, let's say, $500,000 and the market drops 20%, then the losses are $100,000. The question is, will the market recover before you retire? Keep this very important fact in mind. When your dollars are recovering from losses, they are earning zero. This means that the value is eroding due to inflation.

Also, remember what happened in Japan. Our current course is very similar to Japan's was in the 1980's. There is always the possibility that the stock market suffers significant losses and, even after 30 years, never recovers.

Cash value life insurance takes most, if not all the above mentioned risk off the table. You can be certain that you will not participate in market losses ever again. In fact, even in bad economies, markets can have positive years. Imagine not participating in the downside of the market, and yet, have growth when the markets are higher. Talk about the best of both worlds.

Life insurance also eliminates tax risk. Based on what is going on out there, between politics and Government spending, we are very likely to be facing higher taxes in the future. Taxes are the biggest wealth eroders known.

Imagine saving $1,000,000 over the course of your working years, only to have $250,000 or more taken by the tax man. If taxes are higher, those numbers could be drastically worse. You could, in fact, have to pay the IRS and state a total of $400,000 on that million, leaving you with $600,000.

So, let us help you remove that risk and worry from your life once and for all. You deserve to keep most, if not all, the money you saved and earned during your working years. You also deserve to live a retirement free from worry of outliving your money. There are ways to maximize your savings, as mentioned earlier, and a key factor would be to be able to legally avoid handing money over to the IRS.

Remember earlier when I talked about Waiver of Premium? It was during our discussion on how to pay off your home early. Wouldn't that apply here as well? If you are invested in mutual funds that are available to you in your 401(k), what would happen to your retirement savings plans if you were to become disabled?

Not only would your savings cease, but you may have to take loans from that 401(k), that you may or may not ever be able to pay back. With waiver of premium, you can be assured that your savings plan will continue to be funded so that you will not suffer any major gaps in savings.

You may be wondering how to reap the upside of the markets without the downside risk. I totally understand. Allow me to illustrate for you what this scenario could look like, when comparing putting money into a retirement account vs a properly structured cash value life insurance plan. I am going to assume an 11% cap on the indexing strategy.

Indexing is a method that companies utilize to credit interest in some cash value life insurance plans. By crediting in this way, you participate in the upside of the market, with a cap, without participating in losses. While the upside is limited, and there are various ways to index, the chart below shows how much more effective an indexing strategy could be. The beginning balance is $100,000, and these the actual S&P performance numbers:

Year	S&P	Return	Retirement Plan Balance	Return	Indexing Strategy Balance
1999	19.53%	19.53%	$119,530	11%	$111,000
2000	-10.14%	-10.14%	$107,409.66	0.00%	$111,000
2001	-13.04%	-13.04%	$93,403.44	0.00%	$111,000
2002	-23.37%	-23.37%	$71,575.06	0.00%	$111,000
2003	26.38%	26.38%	$90,456.56	11%	$123,210
2004	8.99%	8.99%	$98,588.60	8.99%	$134,286.58
2005	3.00%	3.00%	$101,546.26	3.00%	$138,315.78
2006	13.62%	13.62%	$115,376.86	11%	$153,530.45
2007	3.53%	3.53%	$119,449.66	3.53%	$158,950.08
2008	-38.49%	-38.49%	$73,473.48	0.00%	$158,950.08
2009	23.45%	23.45%	$90,703.01	11%	$176,434.59
2010	12.78%	12.78%	$102,294.86	0.00%	$176,434.59
2011	0.00%	0.00%	$102,294.86	0.00%	$176,434.59
2012	13.41%	13.41%	$116,012.60	11%	$195,842.40
2013	29.60%	29.60%	$150,352.33	11%	$217,385.06
2014	11.39%	11.39%	$167,477.46	11%	$241,297.42
2015	-0.73%	-0.73%	$166,254.87	0.00%	$241,297.42
2016	9.54%	9.54%	$182,115.59	9.54%	$264,317.19
2017	19.42%	19.42%	$217,482.44	11%	$293,392.08
2018	-6.24%	-6.42%	$203,520.07	0.00%	$293,392.08

2019	28.90%	28.90%	$262,337.37	11%	$325,665.21

As you can clearly see, the indexing strategy is far more effective when it comes to building your nest egg. Over this 20 year period, including the biggest bull run in history, indexing outperformed investing directly in the market. By the way, you can look at any 20 year period and indexing will always outperform investing directly in the markets.

Why 20 years though? These are savings right? Isn't this supposed to be about building that nest egg for retirement? There is a reason it is called retirement savings. You aren't supposed to take losses in a savings account. For most people, putting money into a retirement plan is a roll of the dice. How many take the time to understand what is really happening inside of a retirement account?

Also consider, this indexing strategy will allow you to take distributions tax free. This is not the case with a retirement account. Based on the above figures, you can take off at least 20% of the value of the investing direct account, or $52,467.47. This brings the actual account value down to $209,869.90. Oh, and if you believe taxes will be higher in the future, this could easily bring that balance well below $200,000.

This drives home the point that you do not need to ride the Wall St. roller coaster in order to grow wealth. There is no reason to stress out if markets do not perform. I don't care if the markets double again over the next decade. There will still be down years, which an indexing strategy won't participate in. On the flip side, if markets underperform, there will still be years when it is up for the year. It truly is a win-win when it comes to growing your nest egg.

Also, we have clients who want nothing to do with the markets, whether it is investing or indexing. They simply would like a consistent return and take little or no risk. These people typically prefer a high quality whole life policy.

Now, if that same $100,000 was in a properly designed whole life policy, earning 4%, and during that same time period, the money would have grown to $227,876.85. While this looks like less than the investing strategy, it is actually more. Again, with the whole life plan, distributions can be taken tax free.

I hope you understand that we really do not need to be chasing returns. If you can consistently earn interest and/or dividends, your money will most likely outperform any mutual fund you would invest in. Historically, it has. Also, let us not forget, no stress or high blood pressure from market losses. This leads to peace of mind and a higher quality of life.

Chapter 13

Another Income Protection Solution

I've seen this posted on Social Media throughout the years and it makes me chuckle and realize the reality at the same time. It is usually equipped with a funny picture and the quote would read something like this: You insure your phone but not your life?

Think about all the possessions we insure right now. We have homeowners or rental insurance, auto insurance, health insurance, and we even insure our phones. While all are important, necessary, and some even required, why do so few of us consider insuring our income?

Life insurance will protect our income and family's financial well being should we pass away, but what about when we are alive?

This is where a solid income protection plan, or disability policy, comes into play. Think about it for a moment. If your phone is not insured and it breaks, you will have to purchase a new one. Don't get me wrong, phones are getting more expensive by the day and a new Iphone could run you $1,000 or more.

I know that $1,000 can be painful, but what if your

income stopped because you became seriously injured or sick? This could mean losses of $3,000, $4,000, or even as much as $10,000 a month!

While I am not speculating what you earn, I am sure you get where I am going with this. A new Iphone will run you $1,000 one time, but your income would be thousands of dollars every month, until you can return to work.

Are you aware that ⅓ of Americans will become disabled for 90 days or more before age 65? To add to this, the average disability absence is 2 ½ years. Could you afford to have zero, or drastically reduced, income for that period of time?

To put things into perspective for you, a disability is 16 times more likely to cause a foreclosure than a death, and is a leading contributor to individual bankruptcy.

More than 80% of working Americans don't have disability coverage, or are not covered adequately. I am aware that some companies do offer disability, but be aware of what it is you have.

Some things to consider when it comes to group disability. A group disability policy is tied to your employer and if you ever changed jobs, or lost your current job, you cannot take that policy with you.

Another key factor is that if the employer is paying

for the policy, if you ever need it, the income you receive will be taxable. On the flip side, if you own a personal disability plan, you generally pay with after tax dollars, and the income received from this type of plan is tax free.

Something else to keep in mind is that most group disability policies have, what is called, a 90 day elimination period. What this means is that you must be deemed disabled for 90 days prior to benefits kicking in. With personally owned policies, you may choose your elimination period. Typically the longer the elimination period, the lower the premiums.

When you take out a personal disability policy, you will know what your monthly income will be, should you become disabled. With the group plans at work, benefits can range between 50-60% of your income.

This could be devastating as most families are working more and still struggling. So, not only will you be forced to take a drastic pay cut, but there is also nothing you can do about it, as you are disabled.

This chapter is to make you aware of your situation because most people I sit down with, don't understand what they have, when it comes to group disability. By the way, a personally owned Disability policy doesn't have to be super expensive for you either. Just like life insurance, it is all in the plan and design.

When it comes to disability insurance, there are two definitions that companies go by:
- Any Occupation
- Own Occupation

Almost all group disability, and some personally owned plans, will go by the any occupation definition. What this means is that if you were capable of working a different type of job, even if for less money, you would not qualify for benefits. Now, to expand on the definition, it also means that the other job has to be reasonably suited, when it comes to education, age, and experience.

When it comes to one's own occupation, it means just that. For example, if I were a dentist and I became disabled and could not perform my duties as a dentist, I would be eligible to receive benefits. In other words, if you cannot perform your same job, then you qualify.

Benefits periods can range from 2 years, 5 years,10 years, or even to age 65-70, depending on the company. On top of that, companies do place an expiration date on your policy. Typically the policy will end, assuming not already used in full, between the ages of 65-70.

When it comes to life insurance, being approved for a policy usually involves checking the medical and prescription history, height, weight, history of illness, and lifestyle risks, such as smoking.

With disability, all of this is also taken into consideration, and another factor is the type of work you do. For example, someone who works with their hands will pay a higher premium than the person who works at the front desk, assuming all other things are equal.

There are also many ways to enhance your income protection plan, without breaking the bank. There are add ons, also known as riders, that can make all the difference in the world, should you become injured or be diagnosed with a major illness. Like with any person I speak with, I never take a one size fits all approach.

Cost of Living Rider:

Let's face it, prices go up and everyday items get more expensive. On top of that, if all is going well with you, you should get periodic raises at your workplace, or eventually find a place that will pay you more. If you are disabled and have an individually owned policy, your benefits will remain level, for as long as you are receiving benefits.

There is where the cost of living rider can come

into play. If you are disabled beyond one year, your monthly income would increase, for example 3%, the following year, if you had this in place. This is very effective if disabled for a few years, and will help you battle rising costs, so you can focus on what matters most, healing.

Guarantee of Physical Insurability Rider:

By adding this to your income protection plan, you will have the ability to increase your coverage every year, up to age 60. This will give you coverage, based on your added income. In other words, if you receive a wage increase, you can increase your income protection benefit as well.

Also, keep in mind that with this rider, you will not have to show evidence of insurability, only financial proof. In other words, if you are not as healthy as you were when you first took out your income protection plan, the insurance company cannot hold that against you.

Student Loan Reimbursement Rider:

For the majority of people who get a higher education, a mountain of debt is likely to follow them, in the form of student loans. If you never have student loans, congratulations! For the rest of you, this student loan reimbursement rider will ensure that you do not fall behind on your payments, in the event of a disability.

In short, this rider will provide an extra monthly benefit if you are totally disabled to help pay down your student loan obligation. Again, if you are totally disabled, going to work is not an option, so this is another tool to prevent a financial catastrophe.

Chapter 14

In Retirement

When it comes to retirement, what do you think of? The golden years, time to kick back and play golf, or perhaps the opportunity to travel the world? While we all have different goals and dreams, one thing remains constant. If we don't have enough income in retirement to provide, then our reality will be much different than what we always dreamt of.

As I have mentioned earlier, many people near or in retirement are struggling financially. Their top concern is not death, but rather running out of money while alive. You are reading this book at the perfect time because you have the time to help you to never worry about outliving your finances.

I often ask people a simple question. What is more important, asset allocation or income allocation? While the question seems simple enough, the answer often is not.

Many people in their sixties and beyond may turn to CDs as a safe way to preserve their hard earned life savings. The reality is, if you were to put a million dollars in a CD today, you would earn about 2.15%, as of this writing. This equates to $21,500 annually, and this interest is taxable, in most cases. Not sure about you, but I always thought a million dollars would earn me more than that.

For most others, the savings comes in the form of retirement plans, such as a 401(k). With these plans, you are allocating the money into mutual funds. While you may have the opportunity for potential higher growth, what happens when you go to take distributions?

Most old school planners will talk to you about the 4% rule. In other words, if you withdraw 4% a year, your savings should last a lifetime. What they don't tell you is that if you are used to a certain lifestyle and the market goes down, won't that 4% result in a lower income? While you can always take more than 4% to bridge that gap, the risk of running out of money sooner goes dramatically higher.

This rule is a blanket, one size fits all approach. It does not take into consideration your investment objectives or portfolio. In addition, with interest rates so low, and for such an extended period of time, how can one be certain they will earn at least 4% to keep pace with their withdrawals?

This is where annuities come in. Now, annuities are not right for everyone, but for income purposes, can guarantee you will never run out of income, no matter what the markets do. In other words, you take your retirement nest egg, and buy yourself a pension.

Remember pensions? Our grandparents had them, and many of our parents have them as well. That was how it was done, until the 401(k) came along. Today, we must plan for our own retirement and diligently save our money. When you purchase an annuity, you purchase your very own pension plan.

Annuities can also be quite confusing and complicated, and quite frankly, most people, including licensed representatives, do not understand them. So, let me give you some definitions to help give you some clarity.

Immediate Annuity:

With an immediate annuity, the client is trading a lump sum of money for a guaranteed income over a period of time. This period could be for their life, the lives of the life of the client and their spouse, or some other period.

Deferred Annuity:

With a deferred annuity, you would not be seeking an immediate income, but rather, defer that income until a later date. This has two advantages, assuming the income is not needed right away. First, it will grow interest and allow you to take income based on a larger dollar amount. Second, the older you are, the higher percentage of your nest egg you can take annually, as it is based on life expectancy.

Of course, if one was to defer for the higher income, and then pass away, there are ways to make sure that the money is not lost forever. There are ways to name a spouse as a beneficiary or have your spouse continue the income until he or she passes away.

Fixed Annuity:

Fixed annuities offer a fixed interest rate that is typically higher than a CD. Interest rates can vary, usually based on the surrender period.

The surrender period is the amount of time you are willing, and comfortable, locking your money up. Should you have to take money during this time, you could be subject to surrender charges. On that note, most insurance companies do allow for a 10% withdrawal annually, just in case. There are also riders that may allow you to take funds, if truly needed, like in the case of skilled nursing care.

If you put your money into a fixed annuity, with a 3 year surrender, your interest rate may be about 3.2%. That same annuity with a 5 year surrender, may offer a 4.1% interest rate. Basically, the longer you are willing, and able, to tie your money up, the more the insurance company will pay you.

Annuities are never designed for the short term. They are long term instruments and if anyone is going to need access to funds prior to the surrender period ending, should not put that money into an annuity.

Many representatives do a poor job helping their clients understand this, ultimately giving annuities a black eye. It isn't the annuity that is sub par, but rather the person offering it.

Variable Annuity:

Oh, where do I begin with the variable annuity? Okay, let me begin with how they work, then I will share my thoughts on them.

A variable annuity is a deferred annuity, but unlike a fixed annuity, which places your money in an interest bearing account, your money is placed in sub accounts. These sub accounts are mutual funds. This gives the annuitant an opportunity to participate in the upside of the market.

There is also a risk of losing money as well. With these types of annuities, the insurance company is transferring all the risk to the annuitant.

Variable annuities typically come fully equipped with excessive fees, especially when adding riders. Many people who purchase an annuity are doing so for income purposes.

They are sold as the best of both worlds, meaning, get stock market gains and a guaranteed income. What people don't understand are the costs that are involved.

There are fees for the income riders, administrative costs, and since the money is in mutual funds, you are likely paying annual fees there as well. These fees could be costing 3% every year, and like a 401(k), that fee comes out whether you earn or lose money.

This is my problem with variable annuities. Annuities are meant to be safe money and preserve what you worked so hard to build. The last thing anyone needs is to risk that money.

Variable advocates will try and convince you that it doesn't matter because the income is guaranteed. Why all those fees though?

If you want to risk your money in the market, why should you have to pay 3% to do it? It just doesn't make sense. There are more cost effective, much safer options for you.

Indexed Annuities:

Indexed annuities are a great option, if you are seeking to defer and grow your money. One of the pitfalls to indexed annuities is that most of them come with lengthy surrender periods.

Personally, I don't see the problem, assuming you are thinking long term. This could give you a decade or more to further grow your nest egg before taking an income, not that you are required to begin your income stream.

Indexing is a strategy that allows you to participate in the upside of the market without the downside risk. Most of the time, the upside will be capped. What I mean by cap is, you can earn up to 6% for example, then no more. So, if the market was up 10%, your gains would stop at 6%.

On the flip side, if the market was down 10%, you would not lose any money. This is a fair trade off as when one never has to recover from market losses, the money tends to grow faster.

There are different strategies out there, but the most important factor is that you do not lose money if the markets are down. Also, fees are modest. If one puts their money into an indexed annuity simply for growth, the fees could actually be zero. If one is looking to grow for income purposes at a later date, then the fees may still be lower than 1%.

Annuities are designed to create income. If someone has the opportunity to grow their savings, within an annuity, prior to the need to take an income, this is an amazing tool. However, I caution against using a variable annuity as the account value could go lower, depending on market performance.

With all the fixed and indexed annuities available

today, there is little or no need for someone to place their retirement savings within a variable annuity.

Cash Value Life Insurance:

Cash value can play a tremendous role for someone near or in retirement. Many people feel they might be too old for these strategies, but quite the opposite is true.

If you are in retirement, have a nest egg that you don't need income from, and would like to leave to your 2 children, life insurance can all but guarantee that your wishes are met.

Let's say right now these funds are in an IRA, and there is $500,000 total. If you were to pass away tomorrow, each child would get $250,000. Seems simple enough right? Here is where things get a bit more complicated.

If your children were to receive $250,000 each, they would have to pay taxes on every dollar that they take out of that account. In addition, to be in compliance with the Secure Act, which became law on 01/01/2020, all the funds will have to be distributed within a ten year time frame.[17]

If the children took distributions equally over ten years, this would be $25,000 per year. Could an extra $25,000 in reportable income place them in a higher tax bracket? You bet it could. What if they were in a financial bind and needed $50,000 one year? That would raise their taxable income significantly.

Now, if each child received $250,000, taxes would be paid, assuming a total of 25%, in the amount of $125,000. This means that each child would net about $187,500 and the government would receive $125,000. So, if you are following what I am trying to get at, the IRS is getting almost 67% of what your children are getting. Now, imagine if taxes were higher!

But what happens if you don't pass away tomorrow and you live for several more years? Guess what? The IRS has a solution for you here as well.

Beginning at age 72, you will be forced to take required minimum distributions, or RMDs. This means that the longer you live, the more income you will be forced to take, further reducing your account balance. If you don't take the RMDs, you will be faced with a stiff 50% IRS penalty.

What if you needed some kind of skilled nursing care? Are you aware that more than half of people over the age of 65 will need some sort of long term care? The average time that care is needed is about three years. On top of this, the average cost of this care is about $80,000 annually. There are less expensive options available as well as options that may run well north of $100,000 per year.

So, if you have $500,000 and require three years of care, this would reduce your planned inheritance to your children by $240,000. Now your children would receive $260,000 or $130,000 each.

This is where life insurance can come in. You could take that $500,000 and pay into a single premium policy. This could buy you $800,000 of death benefit, depending on age and health, and you would have access to your money, if needed.

Now, if you are in need of that same care, you could access the $240,000, which will reduce your death benefit. When you pass away, you will leave your children a total of about $560,000, and that money will go to them 100% tax free and has zero IRS restrictions or penalties.

Chapter 15

Types Of Cash Value Life Insurance

I hope you realize the power that cash value life insurance can have, when it comes to your financial peace of mind. There are numerous other ways a high quality, properly structured, life insurance plan can benefit you.

There are three main types of cash value life insurance:

- Whole Life
- Variable Universal Life
- Indexed Universal Life

Variable Universal Life:

I want to begin by explaining how variable universal life, or VUL, works. These types of policies are not only the riskiest, but also the most expensive.
Like variable annuities, with VULs, a portion of your premium gets allocated to mutual funds. They are placed in sub accounts, placing all the risk on you.

These kinds of policies are typically sold, under the

guise of higher potential returns, as you would be invested in the stock market. However, after reading through this book, you now clearly understand that exposing your hard earned money in the stock market does not necessarily get you higher returns.

On top of that, you will be paying mutual fund fees annually. Depending on the fund, you could pay north of 1% for any particular fund. Remember, you pay these fees whether the market is up or down. Once again, it is Wall St. that benefits, regardless if you earn or lose money.

Like with retirement accounts, when you are in retirement and it comes time to take distributions, a market downturn during this time could have a dramatic influence on the quality of your retirement. Either you take the same percentage out or you take a larger percent distribution, which will create the risk of running out of money that much sooner.

Many companies do offer a no lapse guarantee, but that makes no sense to me. Why would I pay all those extra premiums for cash value if all I had in the end was a death benefit? Variable life products are just an unnecessary risk.

Whole Life:

Whole life policies are considered the lowest risk, mainly because they offer guarantees. The way cash values grow in a whole life policy are through interest and dividends. However, not all whole life is created equal.

For example, there are mutual companies and there are publicly traded companies. There is a big difference between the two.

With public companies, there are shareholders that are expecting dividends and profits. Therefore, when the insurance company declares a dividend, the shareholders get a piece of the pie as well as you, the policy owner. This could have a significant impact on the cash growth in your account over the long term.

With a mutual company, you are essentially the shareholder. When a dividend is declared, you, the shareholder and policy owner, get the lion's share.

When choosing a whole life, with the purpose of growing your nest egg, you always want to choose a highly rated mutual company, and then make sure it is a participating policy.

When a policy is participating, this will allow you to earn interest and dividends on the entire accumulation value, even if you have a loan outstanding.

Indexed Universal Life:

Indexed Universal Life or IUL, is a very unique type

of policy. Rather than pay dividends, it utilizes an index, like the S&P 500, to grow your cash value.

Like we discussed earlier, an indexing strategy has historically outperformed directly investing into the markets. The main reason being is that you never participate in the downside of the markets. While your upside might be capped, or limited to a certain percentage, it was clearly illustrated in the chapter on saving for retirement, that it grows your money much more effectively than when invested directly.

Chapter 16

Final Thoughts

My motivation for writing this book was to help you understand what is happening out there, both on a large scale as well as your own home. There are so many issues that are being hidden from us, like the real national debt for example.

To make matters worse, Wall St., big banks, and lenders continue to prey on middle America. We pay the highest taxes, have the highest fees, and have the fewest options, oh so you thought.

I hope you now realize that we can all cut the big banks and Wall St. out of our lives. We can also erase a future wealth killer called taxes. I cannot stress enough how much longer your money will last you in retirement and beyond if you are never taxed on those dollars. You can literally flip from being taxed on every future dollar to being never taxed again.

We do not need to risk our money in order to grow it. I have heard time and time again that in order to get the returns we need, our money needs to be handed over to Wall St. bankers and advisors. The time for bankers making money off of our backs, even when we lose money, is done.

There is a quote from the most successful investor that has ever lived, Warren Buffet. He had two simple rules when it came to saving and investing:

1. Never lose money
2. Don't forget rule number one

If we all follow these simple, yet very powerful rules, our financial futures will be brighter than ever.

Here is something to consider as well. Back in 2007-2008, when the great recession hit, it was the banks that needed bailouts. Not one of the highly rated insurance companies required a bailout. This is because banks get your money and leverage it. They use money to lend and borrow more money, and place those funds into riskier investments.

Highly rated insurance companies do not do this, and their financial stability shows that. What blows my mind about the bank bailouts is how the money was used. The big banks gave their executives hefty bonuses, repurchased their own stock to inflate the stock price, and to make matters worse, once again, started making risky investments.

Sure, it is a different world now, but all those banks did was repackage and rename many of these risky investments. After all, these bailouts are from people like you and I, and if they ever crash again, will likely be bailed out again.

On top of that, we will never be paid back those tax dollars that went to the banks and others who received tax payer dollars. Doesn't that make you mad? Not only will we never get it back, but the likelihood of paying much higher income taxes in the near future is a very real concern.

It is my sincerest hope that you gained some real insight and clarification by reading this. All I want is for us to be able to live a life free from financial strains and stress. By taking the Internal Revenue Service, Wall St., and big banks, out of our lives, we can get there!

In closing, if you would like to learn more about how we can help you and your situation, please contact us. There is no cost to chat and never any obligation. Our philosophy is simple when it comes to speaking with potential clients.

If everything we talk about makes sense to you and you decide you would like to work with us, all we ask for is that you implement the plan with us. Outside of that, your only risk with us is just a little bit of your time.

If you are ready to receive your personalized roadmap to financial freedom, here are the ways you may request to chat with one of our highly qualified representatives:

Visit our website & fill out our contact form:

www.polarisfinancialnetwork.com

Call our office: 727-308-3150

or fill out this form, take a picture/scan to this email: info@Polarisfinancialnetwork.com

No Obligation Financial
Roadmap Request Form

Name_____

Best Phone Number_____

Best Time To Reach You

Morning____Afternoon____Evening____

Primary Email:_____

State of Residence_____

Primary Concern (Check all that apply)

Retirement Savings____Retirement Income____

Debt Elimination____Mortgage Acceleration____

College Savings____Income Protection_____

Other_____

We take your privacy very seriously & will never give or sell your information. In addition, all conversations you have with us are strictly confidential.

I would like to take a moment and personally thank you for taking the time to read this book.

I truly hope this was eye opening for you and that you now understand how money operates when it comes to borrowing and saving.

Be sure to follow us on Instagram & Facebook

I would like to thank friends and family who have supported my efforts in writing this book. Means so much to me to have you in my corner.

I would like you to know that I am always available to address any concerns you may have and help you reach your financial goals so that you may live with financial peace of mind.

Sincerely,

Derek Nelson
www.polarisfinancialnetwork.com

727-308-3150

"Derek has dispensed a wealth of information regarding financial issues of the individual within the current economic climate, elaborating the context with valuable examples, and sensible money management solutions." -Dr. Kathleen Shea, Ph.D, Licensed Psychologist

"A passionate advisor that commits whole heartedly to helping families make the right financial decisions" -Jeremy Nason, Insurance Pro Shop

"An exceptionally interesting guide to retirement/financial planning containing a fresh perspective on how to retire comfortably without sacrificing the life you live now." - Michael Caffrey, Mortgage Expert & Financial Advisor

"There is nobody better than Derek Nelson at managing your family's finances. Not only is he an expert in the field, but he cares about each and every family as if it's his own. I highly recommend Derek to lead you in the right direction towards your savings and family's future." - Andrew Scheck, Licensed real estate representative, New York, NY

"I've known Derek Nelson for about 5 years or so. His passion for his work is undeniable! This book, not only outlines the problems that the American Public is facing, but gives some great insights on what we can do to fix it. You'll learn a little more about Derek Nelson's life story – including his time in the NYSE and his "awakening" to search for better ways to manage our personal finances. This is a great book coming from a great guy. You'll enjoy this book. And after you read this book, if you are as bothered by the things going on in our country as I am, then I would also recommend that you contact Derek and see how he can help you gain greater control of your financial future than you thought was possible. Great job, Derek!" - David H. Kinder, ChFC | Chartered Financial Consultant

---

[1] Lending Tree via YouTube https://www.youtube.com/watch?v=3ebAtftMHt0

[2] Wolf of Wall St. movie released 2013 https://www.imdb.com/title/tt0993846/

[3] New York Stock Exchange https://www.nyse.com/index

[4] Stock Market Crash https://en.wikipedia.org/wiki/United_States_bear_market_of_2007%E2%80%932009

[5] Richard Grasso

[6] Walk from Hanover Square to NY Public Library

[7] Japan: https://www.investopedia.com/articles/economics/08/japan-1990s-credit-crunch-liquidity-trap.asp

[8] Pension Debt https://www.forbes.com/sites/chuckdevore/2019/05/31/5-2-trillion-of-government-pension-debt-threatens-to-overwhelm-state-budgets-taxpayers/#6214a22e759d

[9] US Debt Clock https://www.usdebtclock.org/

[10] Pell Grant Information https://studentaid.gov/understand-aid/types/grants/pell

[11] Truth In Accounting Website https://www.truthinaccounting.org/

[12] US Debt Clock https://www.usdebtclock.org/

[13] US Debt Clock https://www.usdebtclock.org/

[14] Stroke Statistics: https://www.cdc.gov/stroke/facts.htm

[15] FDIC details of Bank of America: https://www7.fdic.gov/idasp/advSearchLanding.asp

[16] Top concerns for retirees https://www.marketwatch.com/story/older-people-fear-this-more-than-death-2016-07-18

[17] Secure Act via Marketwatch: https://www.marketwatch.com/story/with-president-trumps-signature-the-secure-act-is-passed-here-are-the-most-important-things-to-know-2019-12-21